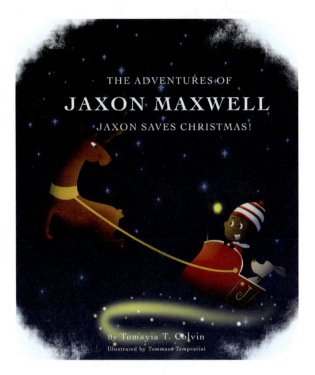

The Adventures of Jaxon Maxwell: Jaxon Saves Christmas!

By: Tomayia T. Colvin
Edited by: Lauren Persons
Illustrated: by Tommaso Tempestini

DEDICATION

Grace & Ivory
Thank you for allowing me to be the best mom, and for always supporting my dreams. This book is for you. Let it always remind you to follow your dreams and to never, ever stop dreaming.
-Mommy

To my parents, brothers, friends, and family, Jaxon Maxwell would not have been possible without your love and support.
Thank you.
Mayia

Copyright © 2016
All rights reserved

Building Literacy Moment!

Parents and teachers, please take a moment to help build your child's reading comprehension before, during, and after reading
The Adventures of Jaxon Maxwell: Jaxon Saves Christmas!

Pre-Reading Questions

What is the title of this book?
Who is the author?
What clues does the title give me about the story?

During Reading Questions

What predictions can I make about Jaxon?
Who is telling the story?
Where does this story take place?
Is this book fiction or nonfiction? How do you know?

After Reading Questions

Why did the author write this story?
How did this story make you feel?
What does the author want you to understand after you have finished reading the story?
How are you alike or different from Jaxon Maxwell?

"It's the most wonderful time of the year!" Jaxon Maxwell said to Mya as they celebrated in Ms. White's class.

"Have a great holiday break!" Ms. White said to her class. The students raced from their classroom to board the bus home.

Jaxon could hardly believe that Christmas was finally here. He waved good-bye to Ms. White and jumped for joy! He knew that he had been especially good this year, and he couldn't wait to mail his letter to Santa! "Honk-honk," the school bus horn said as it drove off.

Jaxon arrived home to find and high five his neighbors, as his dad was in the front yard decorating the house and getting ready for family to come to town. He knew that his mom was busy baking her famous cookies, and he could hardly wait to give them a try.

Jaxon joined his mom in the kitchen, and together they decorated snowman cookies with green, white, and red icing and sprinkles.

"Oh Jax, you are quite the chef my dear! I love when we bake together," his mom said. With Christmas Eve being the next day, Jaxon could hardly contain his excitement.

The next day, Jaxon and his family went to cut down their Christmas tree at the Christmas tree farm, which was a Christmas Eve family tradition. Together, the family selected a beautiful eight foot Douglas Fir.

Just as the family gathered around the television to watch The Polar Express in their pajamas, Jaxon got a sinking feeling in his tummy.

"Oh no," he said to himself. He remembered that he completely forgot to make his parents a special gift to open on Christmas morning.

As everyone else enjoyed movie night, Jaxon sat nervously on the floor, wondering how he could make a gift for his parents by morning. Thankfully, Jaxon knew a few reindeer and elf friends, as he would have to call in a special favor to get to the North Pole.

As snow began to fall outside, Jaxon waited on the reindeer while his family slept. Jaxon and his dog Noah quickly got on the sleigh and headed to Santa's workshop.

"Will I make it back in time before morning?" Jaxon thought to himself as he buckled the seatbelt in the sleigh. "Let's hope so!"

They arrived just in the knick of time at the North Pole!

Jaxon met his elf friends Sarah and Mason at Santa's Workshop in the North Pole. They already knew why he was there, and they worked very hard to make his parents a beautiful handmade clock. Just as they finished, it was almost time to eat breakfast and open gifts.

With the gift in hand, Jaxon quickly flew back home in the sleigh.

He jumped into bed just as his dad was walking in to wake him up for Christmas.

Jaxon smiled joyfully knowing how great it is to have such very thoughtful, helpful, and caring friends.

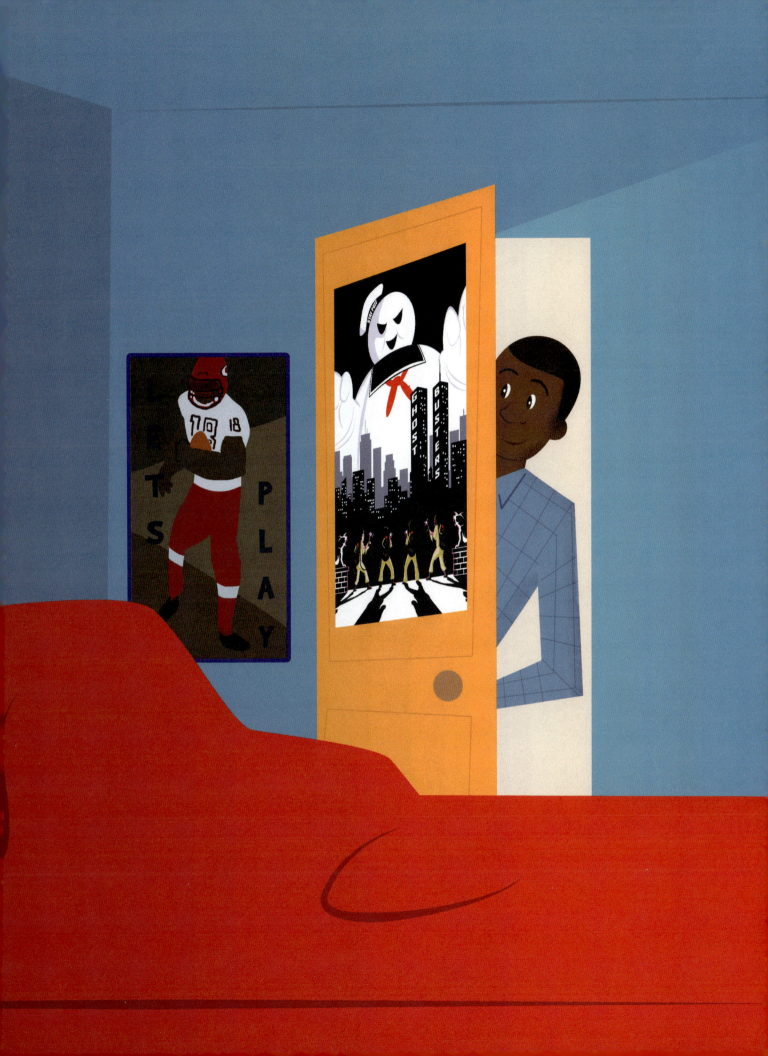

Jaxon was so excited as he raced down the stairs Christmas morning to see his beautifully wrapped clock for his parents underneath the tree!

His mom and dad loved their gift. Jaxon was so excited that this was best Christmas ever and he was able to save Christmas with the help of his friends!

About the Author

Tomayia Colvin is a former educator with 10 years of experience teaching high school and middle school English, Yearbook, and Photography in public schools. She is a high school senior and wedding portrait photographer in Houston, Texas and for the last five years, she has inspired her high school clients to reach their highest potential.

Tomayia has notably been named one of the "50 Most Inspiring Photographers in the United States," with images published in national magazines and blogs such as Essence.Com, Munaluchi Bridal, Black Bride, and Seniorologie. In the fall of 2015, she launched her first solo photography exhibit, The Unboxed Project™, which features the faces of 25 teens redefining the in-crowd and changing the negative stereotypes of teens in the media.

She's also the founder and Editor-in-Chief of Senior Study Hall, a 501(c)3 non-profit organization, that encourages teens to have positive self-esteem. In January 2015, Tomayia was recognized by SYNC Seniors as a trailblazer in the photography community with a passion for giving back to her local community, and inspiring teens and portrait photographers across the globe. Tomayia is a graduate of the University of Houston-Downtown, and obtained a Master of Education in Curriculum & Instruction from Houston Baptist University.

Tomayia is a proud member of Alpha Kappa Alpha Sorority, Incorporated and Jack and Jill of America, Incorporated. She is the mom of two children and resides in Houston, Texas. In her spare time, she enjoys reading, traveling, and spending time with her family.

Connect with the Author

Tomayia Colvin, M.Ed.

www.tomayiacolvin.com
Email: info@tomayiacolvin.com

Facebook: www.facebook.com/myasbigadventures or www.facebook.com/tomayiacolvinphotography

Instagram: www.instagram.com/myasbigadventures

Twitter: www.twitter.com/tomayia

Mail: 9659 N Sam Houston Parkway East 150-285
Humble, Texas 77396

Made in the USA
Charleston, SC
19 December 2016